Night after night, lights burned in the Keller's house in Tuscumbia, Alabama, in the USA. The doctors were afraid Helen would die.

One day the strange illness left – but with it went Helen's **sense** of sight and hearing. Helen had become **blind** and **deaf**. Now that she could no longer hear, she forgot how to speak.

KU-172-842

Helen soon got used to the silent and dark world around her. She used her sense of smell. She made up a **sign language**, so that she could 'talk' with her family. By feeling every object she found she even learned to 'see' with her hands.

Contents

The girl who could see
with her hands   4

Helen finds a friend   9

Annie comes to stay   12

Helen goes to school   16

College days   20

Helen speaks out   22

The work goes on   26

Helen's last gift   28

Glossary   30

Date chart   31

Books to read   31

Index   32

Words printed in **bold** appear in the glossary.

The girl who could see with her hands

Helen as a little girl.

The twenty-seventh of June, 1880, was a very happy day for Captain Keller. His wife Kate had just given birth to a baby girl. They named her Helen. Helen soon grew into a happy and clever child. When she was nineteen months old she was just learning to talk. Then, suddenly, Helen became very ill.

But by the time she was five years old, Helen began to realize that she was different from other people. She could reach out and feel people's lips moving when they talked. But when she tried to copy them, no one could understand her. This made her so angry that she would kick and scream until she was worn out.

All her life, Helen (left) touched people's lips to feel them talking.

When Helen was a child, many people thought that blind people were stupid. Helen's parents loved their daughter and knew she was clever. But even they could see that her temper tantrums made her impossible to control.

Then one of Helen's uncles said they should put her away because she 'was not nice to see' when she was in a temper. Her parents realized they would have to find some help.

Although she could not see or hear, Helen still enjoyed nature. She used her sense of smell.

Helen finds a friend

When Helen was six her parents visited Alexander Graham Bell, the **inventor** of the telephone. They asked him to help them find a school for Helen. Dr Bell knew a lot about teaching deaf people because both his mother and his wife were deaf.

As soon as Helen met Dr Bell, she felt she had found a friend. He held her on his knee and made his pocket watch chime. Helen could feel

When Helen met Alexander Graham Bell she knew she had found a friend.

the **vibrations** through her hands. This made her laugh.

Dr Bell told Captain Keller to write to the director of the Perkins Institution for the Blind,

10

a special school in Boston, to see if he could find a teacher for Helen. The director soon wrote back to say that he had found someone. Her name was Annie Sullivan.

Annie Sullivan was just nineteen years old when she came to teach Helen.

Annie comes to stay

This is the pretty house where Helen was born.

When Annie arrived at the Keller's house she quickly realized that her first job was to tame Helen, who was like a wild child.

Annie took Helen to live with her in a small house in the Keller's garden. At first, this made Helen feel uncertain. Helen had to trust Annie to do

everything for her.
Within two weeks Helen
had learned to obey
Annie, and the two had
become friends.

Whenever Annie gave
something to Helen, she
spelled the name of it
with her finger on to the
back of Helen's hand.
Helen quickly learned to
spell the word back on to
Annie's hand. But she did
not understand that the
words had meanings.

One day Annie held Helen's hand under a water pump. As the water flowed over Helen's hand, Annie traced out the letters W–A–T–E–R. Suddenly Helen understood. Water was the name of the cool thing that was flowing over her hand. She realized that all the

Annie (right) and Helen became lifelong friends.

words Annie spelled on her hand were names of things.

Helen could hardly wait to learn more words. A new exciting world opened up for her – the world of language. To the Kellers, this seemed like a **miracle**.

Helen (back left) met other deaf-blind children at the Perkins Institution.

15

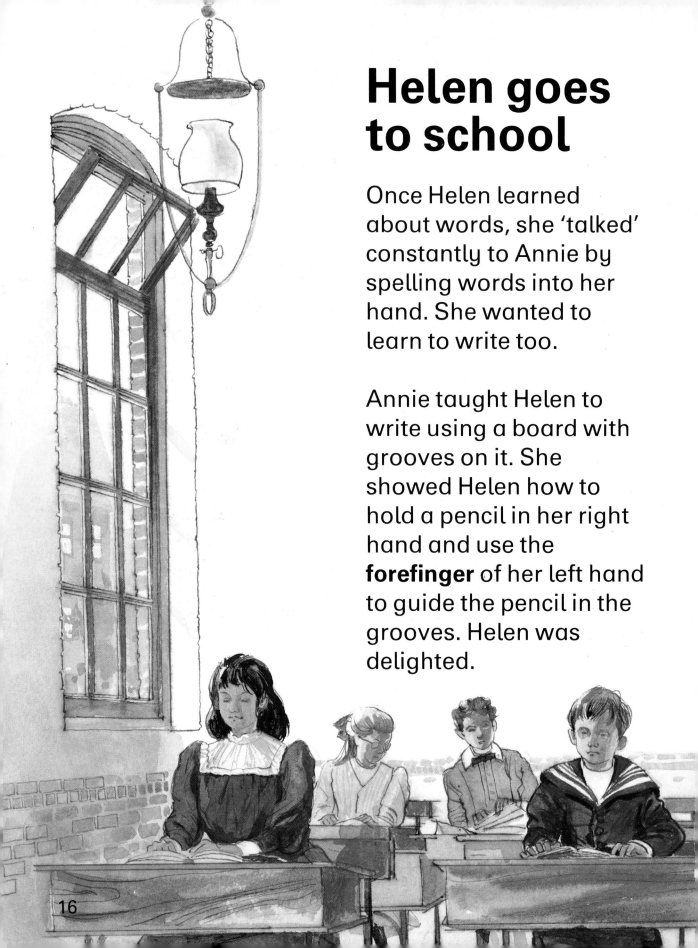

Helen goes to school

Once Helen learned about words, she 'talked' constantly to Annie by spelling words into her hand. She wanted to learn to write too.

Annie taught Helen to write using a board with grooves on it. She showed Helen how to hold a pencil in her right hand and use the **forefinger** of her left hand to guide the pencil in the grooves. Helen was delighted.

So. Boston,
May 1, 1891.

My dear Mr. Brooks;
          Helen sends you a loving greeting this bright May-day. My teacher has just told me that you have been made a bishop, and that your friends everywhere are rejoicing because

Although she could not hear, Helen was used to 'listening' to sounds by feeling vibrations with her **fingertips**. When she realized that words had sounds, she wanted to learn to speak. Annie found a special teacher to teach Helen how to make sounds.

Helen learned to write using a board with grooves on it. This is a letter she wrote.

Below At the Perkins Institution Helen even learnt French and Latin.

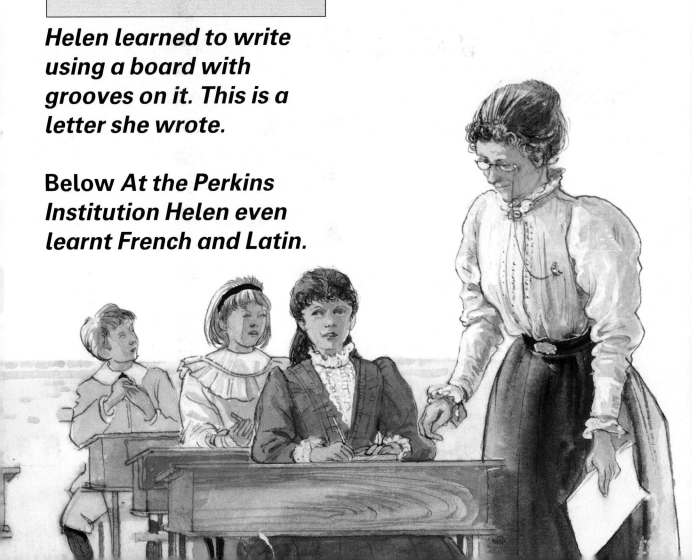

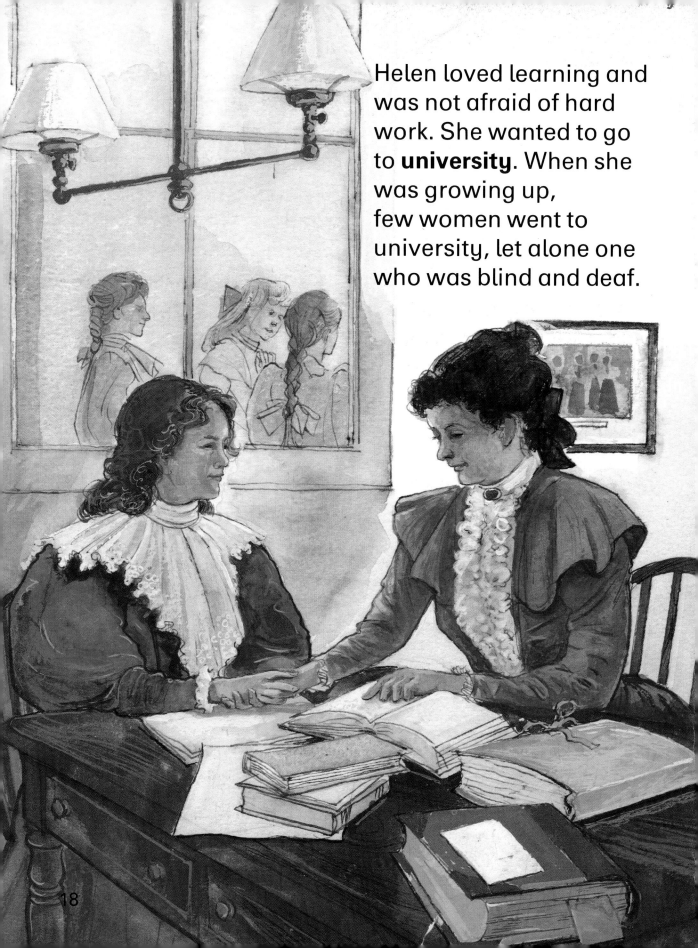

Helen loved learning and was not afraid of hard work. She wanted to go to **university**. When she was growing up, few women went to university, let alone one who was blind and deaf.

Books printed in Braille use a system of raised dots on paper so that blind people can read with their fingers.

But this did not stop Helen. She set her sights on Radcliffe College, a famous university for women.

To prepare for the entrance examination, Helen had to study at a school that was not just for blind or deaf children. There were no special teachers. Helen 'listened' and 'read' with the help of Annie spelling into her hand. She also learned to read Braille. This uses raised dots on paper so that blind people can read with their fingers.

Helen had to work very hard just to keep up. But her hard work paid off. She passed her exams. In the autumn of 1900 Helen entered Radcliffe.

Annie often 'read' to Helen by spelling words into her hand.

College days

At college, Helen worked hard at her studies. Annie spelled the **lectures** and books into her hand and Helen soaked up information like a sponge.

When Helen was not studying, she enjoyed canoeing and sailing with her college friends. She also wrote a book called *The Story of My Life*. The book made Helen famous.

Helen **graduated** from Radcliffe with honours in 1904. She now knew that she could do anything she set her mind to. She decided she would work to help blind and deaf people.

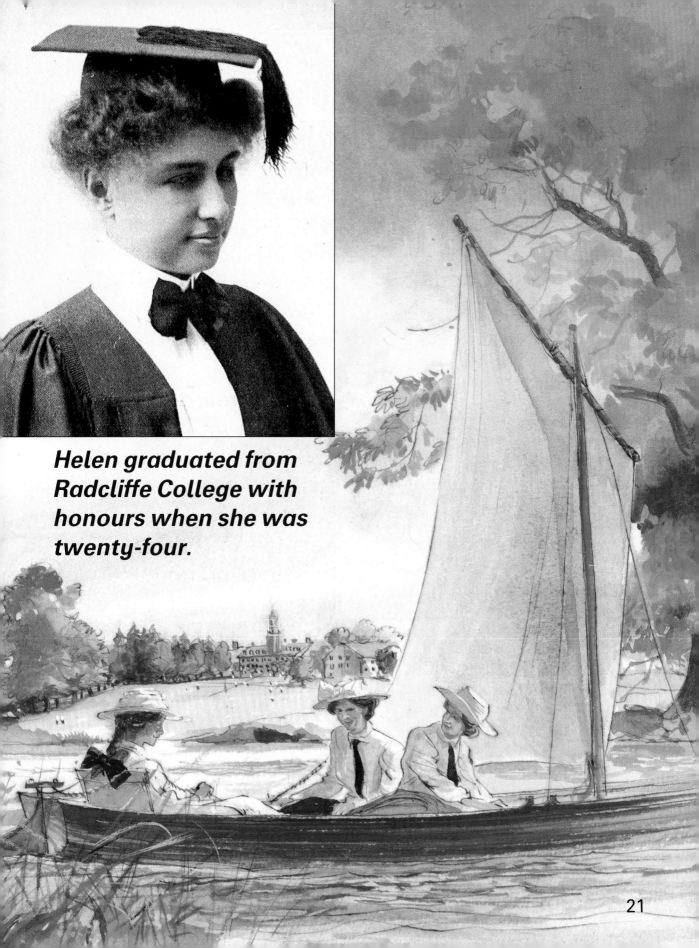

Helen graduated from Radcliffe College with honours when she was twenty-four.

Helen speaks out

Helen began by writing about blindness for magazines. Soon people all over the world were writing to her asking for information about the blind and their needs.

In order to reach even more people, Helen decided to give public lectures about blindness. First she had to work hard to learn to speak more clearly. By 1914, just ten years after she left university, Helen and Annie were giving

A LECTURE
MISS
HELEN
KELLER
7.3

Helen wanted to help blind and deaf people. She began by writing about blindness for magazines.

lectures all over the USA. A young Scottish girl, Polly Thomson, came along to help. Soon the three were good friends.

Helen was also interested in **politics**. She thought women should be allowed to **vote**, which they could not do in the USA before 1920. She thought children should not be made to work. These things made Helen angry and she spoke out about them whenever she could.

In 1921, the American Foundation for the Blind was set up. This foundation asked Helen to go on lecture tours to help raise money. Together with Annie and Polly, Helen took on this important job.

The lecture tours were very hard work, but they were very useful. During these tours Helen met many famous people, even two Presidents of the USA, Herbert Hoover and Franklin Roosevelt. She also met many ordinary people, who found out about the problems of the blind and wanted to help.

Like Helen, President Roosevelt had suffered a terrible illness. He had difficulty walking.

In 1932, Helen, Annie and Polly went on their first lecture tour to Europe. Everywhere they went they were treated as special guests.

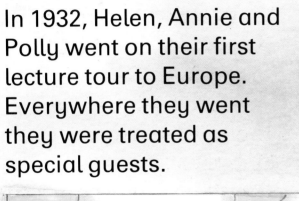

Ireland
Britain
France
Yugoslavia
New York

The work goes on

The three friends enjoyed their travels abroad, but a dark cloud hung over their trip. Annie was ill, and was losing her sight. When Annie died in 1936,

Helen and her helper Polly Thomson (right).

Helen thought her heart would break. But she carried on working. One year after Annie's death, Helen and Polly went on their greatest adventure – a trip to Japan.

In those days the Japanese thought that the gods gave people their **disabilities** and no one could help them. But after Helen's visit, they changed their minds. They set up schemes to help the disabled.

During the **Second World War** Helen visited injured soldiers. She gave hope to people made blind by the fighting.

Even Queen Elizabeth, now the Queen Mother, said that she took **courage** during the war from Helen's example.

Queen Elizabeth, now the Queen Mother, comforted people whose houses were bombed during the war.

Helen's last gift

Above _Helen at seventy._

By 1957, Helen and Polly were too old to go on travelling. They went to live in Westport, Connecticut, but they did not stop working. Helen wanted to write a book about Annie. Writing the book was Helen's way of saying thank you for all Annie had done. She called the book _Teacher_.

Below _Today there are schools for the blind and deaf._

Polly died in 1960, and Helen, too, was becoming very weak. Soon she could no longer work. On 1 June, 1968, just a few weeks before her eighty-eighth birthday, Helen died.

During her long and happy life Helen worked hard to improve the world. The little girl who grew up in a world of darkness and silence left behind the gift of hope and courage for disabled people everywhere.

Glossary

Blind Unable to see.

Courage The strength to face up to problems.

Deaf Unable to hear.

Disabilities Problems which make it hard for a person to do things, for example, not being able to see or not being able to walk.

Fingertips The ends of your fingers, which are very sensitive.

Forefinger The first finger on your hand, the one you point with.

Graduate To leave college after passing your final exams.

Inventor A person who thinks up a new machine.

Lectures Talks given to groups of people.

Miracle A wonderful happening which did not seem possible.

Politics Ideas about how countries should be ruled.

Second World War The fighting that broke out in many parts of the world between 1939 and 1945.

Sense One of the five ways we know about the world around us. They are seeing, hearing, smelling, tasting and touching.

Sign language A way of 'talking' using movements instead of speaking.

University A place where people study when they have left school.

Vibrations Small movements.

Vote To have a say in who is chosen to rule a country.

Date chart

1880 Helen born on 27 June.

1882 Helen has strange illness. Becomes blind and deaf.

1886 Meets Alexander Graham Bell.

1887 Annie Sullivan starts as Helen's teacher.

1896 Helen goes to school to study for college exams.

1900 Enters Radcliffe College.

1903 Writes *The Story of My Life*.

1904 Graduates from Radcliffe. Starts work for the blind.

1921 American Foundation for the Blind set up.

1932 Visits Europe.

1936 Annie dies.

1937 Visits Japan.

1960 Polly Thomson dies.

1968 Helen dies on 1 June.

Books to read

Early 20th Century by Ruth Thomson (Franklin Watts, 1989)

Helen Keller by Nigel Hunter (Wayland, 1985)

I Am Blind by Brenda Pettenuzzo (Franklin Watts, 1988)

I Am Deaf by Brenda Pettenuzzo (Franklin Watts, 1987)

Sally Can't See by Palle Peterson (A & C Black, 1976)

Talk To Me by S. Brearley (A & C Black, 1989)

Index

American Foundation for
   the Blind 24

Bell, Alexander Graham
   9, 10
Boston 11
Braille 19

Elizabeth, Queen (the
   Queen Mother) 27
Europe 25

graduation 20, 21

Hoover, Herbert 24

Japan 26-7

Keller, Helen
   birth 4
   illness 4
   schooling 16-19
   college 20-21
   books 20, 28
   lecture tours 22-7
   death 29

Perkins Institution for the
   Blind 10, 15, 17

Radcliffe College 19-21
Roosevelt, Franklin 24

schools 16-19, 28
Second World War 27
sign language 6
Story of My Life, The 20
Sullivan, Annie 11
   starts as teacher 12
   death 26

Teacher 28
Thomson, Polly, 23-9
Tuscumbia, Alabama 5

Westport, Connecticut 28

Picture acknowledgements
The publishers would like to thank the
following for allowing their pictures to be
reproduced in this book: Mary Evans
Picture Library 15 (top), 21; Hulton-
Deutsch Collection 7, 8, 9, 27 (bottom);
Peter Newark's American Pictures cover,
4, 17, 19 (bottom), 23, 24; Photri 12;
Topham Picture Library 27 (top), 28 (top);
Wayland Picture Library 11, 15 (bottom);
Zefa 19 (top), 28 (bottom).